Learn the Biology Wisdom from Holly Bible

(English & Chinese Bilingual Version)

Learn the Biology Wisdom from Holly Bible

(English & Chinese Bilingual Version)

Chien Min Kuo

Author Biography

Kuo Chien Min was born in Taiwan and became permanent resident of U.S.A. in 2020. He became a Christian when he was 20 years old. He owns the B.S., M.S. and Ph.D. degrees in the field of information management. He ever served as the positions of second lieutenant, programmer, assistant researcher, assistant professor and associate professor in the past. He published 21 peer-reviewed articles in the leading journals, including Information Sciences, Program, the Electronic Library and so on. And, 44 articles published in academic conference proceedings. He also owned over 350 patens in Taiwan, China and USA. He has authored several books such as "The analysis and introduction of English core journal and thesis between 1998 to 2008", "Apply biology to business administration", and so on.

Preface

Holy Bible is the most important and best-selling book in the whole world. There are many creatures mentioned in Bible. In this book, some animals, plants and insects were chosen and selected from bible in order to learn their wisdoms and put them into practice in our daily life.

There are some smart creatures such as ant, coney rabbit, lizard, locust, horse, wild donkey and so on. People can learn from their wisdoms by their characters and living ways given by LORD. There are some stupid or bad living beings such as ostrich and weed which people can learn from their lessons to avoid doing the same stupid or bad things. From good examples, people can learn good models and behaviors. However, people can also learn good lessons from poor models or examples too. All you can do is prevent doing the same stupid and bad behaviors in order to turn stupid into wisdom.

There are two languages' descriptions for every story. Readers can choose their preferred language or learn another language at the same time. In addition, one simple app can be downloaded from Google play store. Please refer to the appendix in this book for it. I am deeply hoped that this can lead people to gain more and more wisdoms in our daily life.

In addition, reader can think two important questions by yourself. Firstly, what kind of person do you want to be or not want to be? Secondly, what kind of person is around you? These means what kind of animal's character.

Chien Min Kuo,   September, 30, 2020

Table of Content

Copyright

Preface

Chapter I. Horse

Chapter II. Eagle

Chapter III. Hippo

Chapter IV. Four Small Creatures

Chapter V. Ostrich

Chapter VI. Wild OX

Chapter VII. Wild Donkey

Chapter VIII. Weeds Parable

Chapter IX. Sower Parable

CHAPTER I. **Horse**

The Lord Answers Job - Horse Topic
-Job 38:1-2,39:19-25 (GNT)Good News Translation
1. Then out of the storm the Lord spoke to Job.
2. Who are you to question my wisdom
   with your ignorant, empty words?
3. Was it you, Job, who made horses so strong
   and gave them their flowing manes?
4. Did you make them leap like locusts
   and frighten people with their snorting?
5. They eagerly paw the ground in the valley;
   they rush into battle with all their strength.
6. They do not know the meaning of fear,
   and no sword can turn them back.
7. The weapons which their riders carry
   rattle and flash in the sun.
8. Trembling with excitement, the horses race ahead;
   when the trumpet blows, they can't stand still.
9. At each blast of the trumpet they snort;
   they can smell a battle before they get near,
   and they hear the officers shouting commands.

The Lord Answers Job - Horse Topic
-Job 38:1-2,39:19-25 (NIV)New International Version
1. Then the Lord spoke to Job out of the storm. He said:
2. Who is this that obscures my plans with words without knowledge?
3. Do you give the horse its strength or clothe its neck with a flowing mane?
4. Do you make it leap like a locust, striking terror with its proud snorting?
5. It paws fiercely, rejoicing in its strength, and charges into the fray.
6. It laughs at fear, afraid of nothing; it does not shy away from the sword.
7. The quiver rattles against its side, along with the flashing spear and lance.
8. In frenzied excitement it eats up the ground; it cannot stand still when the trumpet sounds.
9. At the blast of the trumpet it snorts, 'Aha!'It catches the scent of battle from afar, the shout of commanders and the battle cry.

約伯記 38:1-2, 39:19-25 （CUVMPT）
Chinese Union Version Modern Punctuation
(Traditional)
1. 那時，耶和華從旋風中回答約伯說：
2. 誰用無知的言語，使我的旨意暗昧不明？
3. 馬的大力是你所賜的嗎？牠頸項上挓挲的鬃是你給牠披
上的嗎？
4. 是你叫牠跳躍像蝗蟲嗎？牠噴氣之威使人驚惶。
5. 牠在谷中刨地，自喜其力，牠出去迎接佩帶兵器的人。
6. 牠嗤笑可怕的事並不驚惶，也不因刀劍退回。
7. 箭袋和發亮的槍並短槍，在牠身上錚錚有聲。
8. 牠發猛烈的怒氣將地吞下，一聽角聲就不耐站立。
9. 角每發聲，牠說『呵哈』，牠從遠處聞著戰氣，
又聽見軍長大發雷聲和兵丁吶喊。

约伯记 38:1-2,39:19-25 (CCB)
Chinese Contemporary Bible (Simplified)
1. 那时，耶和华从旋风中回答约伯说：
2. 是是谁用无知的话蒙蔽我的旨意？
3. 马的力量岂是你赐的？
它颈上的鬃毛岂是你披的？
4. 岂是你使它跳跃如蝗虫，发出令人胆寒的长嘶？
5. 它在谷中刨地，炫耀力量，奋力冲向敌军。
6. 它嘲笑恐惧，毫不害怕，不因刀剑而退缩。
7. 它背上的箭袋铮铮作响，长矛和投枪闪闪发光。
8. 角声一响，它便无法静立，狂烈地颤抖，急于驰骋大地。

9. 听到角声，它就发出长嘶，它老远便嗅到战争的气味，
并听见呐喊和将领的号令。

1. Then the Lord spoke to Job out of the storm. He said:

1. 那時，耶和華從旋風中回答約伯說：

2. Who is this that obscures my plans with words without knowledge?

2. 誰用無知的言語，使我的旨意暗昧不明？

3. Do you give the horse its strength or clothe its neck with a flowing mane?

3. 馬的大力是你所賜的嗎？牠頸項上挓挲的鬃是你給牠披上的嗎？

4. Do you make it leap like a locust, striking terror with its proud snorting?

4. 是你叫牠跳躍像蝗蟲嗎？牠噴氣之威使人驚惶。

5. It paws fiercely, rejoicing in its strength, and charges into the fray.

5. 牠在谷中刨地，自喜其力，牠出去迎接佩帶兵器的人。

6. It laughs at fear, afraid of nothing; it does not shy away from the sword.

6. 牠嗤笑可怕的事並不驚惶，也不因刀劍退回。

7. The quiver rattles against its side, along with the flashing spear and lance.

7. 箭袋和發亮的槍並短槍，在牠身上錚錚有聲。

8. In frenzied excitement it eats up the ground; it cannot stand still when the trumpet sounds.

8. 牠發猛烈的怒氣將地吞下，一聽角聲就不耐站立。

9. At the blast of the trumpet it snorts, 'Aha!' It catches the scent of battle from afar, the shout of commanders and the battle cry.

9. 角每發聲，牠說『呵哈』，牠從遠處聞著戰氣，又聽見軍長大發雷聲和兵丁吶喊。

Analysis and Discussion

Characters of Horse

-No fear war

-No fear sword

-Obey the command of human being

-Passion to run

-Inspired by horn

Lessons can be learnt by human being

-Not afraid of enemy or wicked person

-Obey the command of supervisor

-Do not criticize the supervisor

-Passion to perform for the talented skill

-Enthusiasm for interesting habit

-Use right music to stimulate mood

整理與探討

- 馬的特色
  - 對戰爭不恐懼
  - 對刀劍不恐懼
  - 少數動物裡會聽人類命令行事
  - 對跑步有熱情
  - 號角聲會激發其熱情
- 人們可學習的地方(學習哲學)
  - 對敵人或不義的人不畏懼
  - 對主管的命令服從,不批評主管
  - 對有天份的專長有熱情
  - 對有興趣的事有熱情
  - 音樂會影響情緒

CHAPTER II. **Eagle**

The Lord Answers Job - Eagle Topic

-Job 39:26-30 (NIV)(New International Version)

1. Does the hawk take flight by your wisdom

   and spread its wings toward the south?

2. Does the eagle soar at your command

   and build its nest on high?

3. It dwells on a cliff and stays there at night;

   a rocky crag is its stronghold.

4. From there it looks for food;

   its eyes detect it from afar.

5. Its young ones feast on blood,

   and where the slain are, there it is.

The Lord Answers Job - Eagle Topic

-Job 39:26-30 (GNT)(Good News Translation)

1. Does a hawk learn from you how to fly

    when it spreads its wings toward the south?

2. Does an eagle wait for your command

    to build its nest high in the mountains?

3. It makes its home on the highest rocks

    and makes the sharp peaks its fortress.

4. From there it watches near and far

    for something to kill and eat.

5. Around dead bodies the eagles gather,

    and the young eagles drink the blood.

約伯記 39:26-30(CUVMPT)

Chinese Union Version Modern Punctuation (Traditional)

1. 鷹雀飛翔，展開翅膀一直向南，豈是藉你的智慧嗎？

2. 大鷹上騰在高處搭窩，豈是聽你的吩咐嗎？

3. 牠住在山巖，以山峰和堅固之所為家，

4. 從那裡窺看食物，眼睛遠遠觀望。

5. 牠的雛也咂血；被殺的人在哪裡，牠也在哪裡。

约伯记 39:26-30(CCB)

Chinese Contemporary Bible (Simplified)

1. 鹰隼展翅翱翔，飞往南方，

岂是靠你的智慧？

2. 秃鹰腾飞，在高处搭窝，

岂是奉你的命令？

3. 它居住在悬崖上，

盘踞在山岩峭壁，

4. 它从那里搜寻猎物，

它的目光直达远方。

5. 它的幼雏噬血，

哪里有尸体，它就在哪里。

1. Does the hawk take flight by your wisdom

 and spread its wings toward the south?

1. 鷹雀飛翔，展開翅膀一直向南，豈是藉你的智慧嗎？

2. Does the eagle soar at your command

and build its nest on high?

2. 大鷹上騰在高處搭窩，豈是聽你的吩咐嗎？

3. It dwells on a cliff and stays there at night;

a rocky crag is its stronghold.

3. 牠住在山巖，以山峰和堅固之所為家

4. From there it looks for food;

   its eyes detect it from afar.

4. 從那裡窺看食物，眼睛遠遠觀望。

5. Its young ones feast on blood,

   and where the slain are, there it is.

5. 牠的雛也咂血；被殺的人在哪裡，牠也在哪裡。

老鷹的特色

-常從遠處觀望與偵測食物

-住在高山巖,夜間待巢

-築巢在磐石上

人們可學習的地方(學習哲學)

-高處不勝寒

-凡事嘗試用遠見看未來發展

-選擇安全地方蓋房子(高處且磐石穩)

-尋找人生中各種磐石,如朋友,方法(讀書技巧,考試技巧..)等

Characters of Eagle

-Detect food from afar and high.

-Dwell on a cliff and stay there at night.

-Build nest on a rocky crag.

Lessons can be learnt by human being

-Try to look everything far away for the future.

-Choose safe place to build house (High and Rock).

-Look for all kinds of rocks in life,

ex: good friends, solutions (study skill, exam skill..) and so on.

Characters of Eagle

-Detect food from afar and high.
-Dwell on a cliff and stay there at night.
-Build nest on a rocky crag.

Lessons can be learnt by human being

-Try to look everything far away for the future.
-Choose safe place to build house (High and Rock).
-Look for all kinds of rocks in life,
ex: good friends, solutions (study skill, exam skill..) and so on.

老鷹的特色

-常從遠處觀望與偵測食物

-住在高山巖,夜間待巢

-築巢在磐石上

人們可學習的地方(學習哲學)

-高處不勝寒

-凡事嘗試用遠見看未來發展

-選擇安全地方蓋房子(高處且磐石穩)

-尋找人生中各種磐石,如朋友,方法(讀書技巧,考試技

巧..)等

CHAPTER III. **Hippo**

-Job 40:15-24 (New International Version)

The Lord Answers Job - Hippo Topic

1. Look at Behemoth, which I made along with

you and which feeds on grass like an ox.

2. What strength it has in its loins,

    what power in the muscles of its belly!

3. Its tail sways like a cedar;

    the sinews of its thighs are close-knit.

4. Its bones are tubes of bronze, its limbs like rods of iron.

5. It ranks first among the works of God,

    yet its Maker can approach it with his sword.

6. The hills bring it their produce,

    and all the wild animals play nearby.

7. Under the lotus plants it lies,

    hidden among the reeds in the marsh.

8. The lotuses conceal it in their shadow;

    the poplars by the stream surround it.

9. A raging river does not alarm it; it is secure,

though the Jordan should surge against its mouth.

10. Can anyone capture it by the eyes, or trap it and pierce its nose?

-Job 40:15-24 (Good News Translation)

The Lord Answers Job - Hippo Topic

1. Look at the monster Behemoth;

   I created him and I created you.

2. He eats grass like a cow, but what strength there is in his body,

   and what power there is in his muscles!

3. His tail stands up like a cedar,

   and the muscles in his legs are strong.

4. His bones are as strong as bronze,

   and his legs are like iron bars.

5. The most amazing of all my creatures!

   Only his Creator can defeat him.

6. Grass to feed him grow son the hills where wild beasts play.

7. He lies down under the thorn bushes,

   and hides among the reeds in the swamp.

8. The thorn bushes and the willows by the stream

   give him shelter in their shade.

9. He is not afraid of a rushing river;

   he is calm when the Jordan dashes in his face.

10. Who can blind his eyes and capture him?

約伯記 40:15-24(CUVMPT)

Chinese Union Version Modern Punctuation (Traditional)

耶和華以造物之妙詰約伯-河馬篇

1. 你且觀看河馬，我造你也造牠，牠吃草與牛一樣。

2. 牠的氣力在腰間，能力在肚腹的筋上。

3. 牠搖動尾巴如香柏樹，牠大腿的筋互相聯絡。

4. 牠的骨頭好像銅管，牠的肢體彷彿鐵棍。

5. 牠在神所造的物中為首，創造牠的給牠刀劍。

6. 諸山給牠出食物，也是百獸遊玩之處。

7. 牠伏在蓮葉之下，臥在蘆葦隱密處和水窪子裡。

8. 蓮葉的陰涼遮蔽牠，溪旁的柳樹環繞牠。

9. 河水氾濫，牠不發戰，就是約旦河的水漲到牠口邊，也是安然。

10. 在牠防備的時候，誰能捉拿牠？誰能牢籠牠，穿牠的鼻子呢？

约伯记 40:15-24(CCB)

Chinese Contemporary Bible (Simplified)

1. 你看河马，它和你都是我造的，它像牛一样吃草。

2. 你看它腰间的气力，它腹部肌肉的力量。

3. 它尾巴挺直如香柏树，大腿的筋紧密相连，

4. 骨头如铜管，四肢像铁棍。

5. 它是上帝创造的杰作，创造主赐给它利刃。

6. 群山供应它食物，百兽在那里玩耍。

7. 它躺在莲叶之下，藏在泥沼的芦苇间，

8. 莲叶为它遮荫，溪畔的柳树环绕它。

9. 河水泛滥，它不惊惧；约旦河涨到它口边，它也无忧。

10. 谁能在它警觉时捕捉它，或用钩子穿透它的鼻子？

1. Look at Behemoth, which I made along with

   you and which feeds on grass like an ox.

1. 你且觀看河馬，我造你也造牠，牠吃草與牛一樣。

2. What strength it has in its loins,

   what power in the muscles of its belly!

2. 牠的氣力在腰間，能力在肚腹的筋上。

3. His tail stands up like a cedar,

and the muscles in his legs are strong.

3. 牠搖動尾巴如香柏樹，牠大腿的筋互相聯絡。

4. His bones are as strong as bronze,

   and his legs are like iron bars.

4. 牠的骨頭好像銅管，牠的肢體彷彿鐵棍。

5. The most amazing of all my creatures!

   Only his Creator can defeat him.

5. 牠在神所造的物中為首，創造牠的給牠刀劍。

6. Grass to feed him grows on the hills where wild beasts play.

6. 諸山給牠出食物，也是百獸遊玩之處。

7. He lies down under the thorn bushes,

   and hides among the reeds in the swamp.

7. 牠伏在蓮葉之下，臥在蘆葦隱密處和水窪子裡。

8. The thorn bushes and the willows by the stream

   give him shelter in their shade.

8. 蓮葉的陰涼遮蔽牠，溪旁的柳樹環繞牠。

9. He is not afraid of a rushing river;

he is calm when the Jordan dashes in his face.

9. 河水氾濫，牠不發戰，就是約旦河的水漲到牠口邊，也是安然。

10. Who can blind his eyes and capture him?

10. 在牠防備的時候，誰能捉拿牠？誰能牢籠牠，穿牠的鼻子呢？

河馬的特色

-強壯且具力量, 但卻友善。

-不害怕河水氾濫。

-保持冷靜, 即使河水漲到嘴邊。

-吃綠草如公牛。

-伏在蓮葉之下，臥在蘆葦隱密處和水窪子裡。

-骨頭強壯如銅, 腳壯如鐵柱。

人們可學習的地方(學習哲學)

-面對災難, 具備知識。

-植物是每個人的好朋友, 即使是孔武有力的生物。

-遮蔽物與躲藏處是每個人都會需要。

-躲藏在 神的羽翼下。

Characters of Hippo

-Strongly and powerfully, but friendly.

-Not afraid of a rushing river.

-Keep calm when river dashes in his face.

-Eat grass like an ox.

-Lie down under the thorn bushes and hide among the reeds in the swamp.

-Bones are as strong as bronze and legs are like iron bars.

Lessons can be learnt by human being

-Have knowledge to deal with disaster.

-Plant is good friend for everyone, even the powerful creature.

-Shadow and Hidden place is necessary for everyone.

-Hide under the wing of GOD.

河馬的特色

-強壯且具力量,但卻友善。

-不害怕河水氾濫。

-保持冷靜,即使河水漲到嘴邊。

-吃綠草如公牛。

-伏在蓮葉之下,臥在蘆葦隱密處和水窪子裡。

-骨頭強壯如銅,腳壯如鐵柱。

人們可學習的地方（學習哲學）

-面對災難,具備知識。

-植物是每個人的好朋友,即使是孔武有力的生物。

-遮蔽物與躲藏處是每個人都會需要。

-躲藏在 神的羽翼下。

Characters of Hippo

-Strongly and powerfully, but friendly.
-Not afraid of a rushing river.
-Keep calm when river dashes in his face.
-Eat grass like an ox.
-Lie down under the thorn bushes and hide among the reeds in the swamp.
-Bones are as strong as bronze and legs are like iron bars.

Lessons can be learnt by human being

-Have knowledge to deal with disaster.
-Plant is good friend for everyone, even the powerful creature.
-Shadow and Hidden place is necessary for everyone.
-Hide under the wing of GOD.

CHAPTER IV. **Four Small Creatures**

Four Extremely Wise Small Creatures

-Proverbs 30:24-28(NIV)(New International Version)

1. Four things on earth are small,
   yet they are extremely wise:
2. Ants are creatures of little strength,
   yet they store up their food in the summer;
3. hyraxes are creatures of little power,
   yet they make their home in the crags;
4. locusts have no king,
   yet they advance together in ranks;
5. a lizard can be caught with the hand,
   yet it is found in kings' palaces.

Four Extremely Wise Small Creatures
-Proverbs 30:24-28 (GNT)(Good News Translation)

1. There are four animals in the world that are small,
but very, very clever:
2. Ants: they are weak, but they store up their food in the
summer.
3. Rock badgers: they are not strong either,
but they make their homes among the rocks.
4. Locusts: they have no king, but they move in formation.
5. Lizards: you can hold one in your hand, but you can find
them in palaces.

四種極聰明的小生物
-箴言 30:24-28(CUVMPT)

Chinese Union Version Modern Punctuation (Traditional)
1. 地上有四樣小物，卻甚聰明：
2. 螞蟻是無力之類，卻在夏天預備糧食；
3. 沙番(岩蹄兔)是軟弱之類，卻在磐石中造房；
4. 蝗蟲沒有君王，卻分隊而出；
5. 守宮用爪抓牆，卻住在王宮。

四种极聪明的小生物
-箴言 30:24-28 (CCB)

Chinese Contemporary Bible (Simplified)

1. 地上有四种动物，身体虽小却极其聪明：
2. 蚂蚁力量虽小，却在夏天储备粮食；
3. 石獾虽不强壮，却在岩石中筑巢穴；
4. 蝗虫虽无君王，却整齐地列队前进；
5. 壁虎虽易捕捉，却居住在王宫大内。

1. Four things on earth are small,

   yet they are extremely wise:

1. 地上有四樣小物，卻甚聰明：

2. Ants are creatures of little strength,

   yet they store up their food in the summer;

2. 螞蟻是無力之類，卻在夏天預備糧食；

3. Hyraxes are creatures of little power,

   yet they make their home in the crags;

3. 沙番（岩蹄兔）是軟弱之類，卻在磐石中造房；

4. Locusts have no king,

   yet they advance together in ranks;

4. 蝗蟲沒有君王，卻分隊而出；

5. A lizard can be caught with the hand,

  yet it is found in kings' palaces.

5. 守宮用爪抓牆，卻住在王宮。

螞蟻的特色

- 體型微小暨力氣微小

- 勤奮、勤勞

- 在夏日儲存糧食

- 團隊合作

- 階層式結構

- 使用化學物質攻擊敵人

- 在我們週遭環境無所不在

人們可學習的地方（學習哲學）

- 工作努力 & 不偷懶

- 找出不同事件的冬天並且儘早準備（例：考試日期，專案截
止日等）

- 樂於與他人合作進而產生良好團隊

- 在每個工作崗位上善盡職責

- 待人有禮

- 先求無所不在，再求獲利

Characters of Ants

- Small & little strength

- Diligent

- Store up food in the summer

- Teamwork

- Hierarchical structure

- Use chemical compound to attack enemy or leave message

- They are ubiquitous in our environment.

Lessons can be learnt by human being

- Work hard & Not lazy

- Identify what is our winter and prepare it early (Ex: exam date, project deadline and so on.)

- Cooperate with others to become a good team

- Play the role and do job well in the current position.

- Polite to contact with others

- Ubiquitous firstly, then profit.

沙番（岩蹄兔）的特色

- 軟弱的生物

- 把家蓋在磐石中

人們可學習的地方（學習哲學）

-尋找出人生中的每一項磐石, 如真神, 聖經, 益友, 考試技巧, 學習技巧, 工作技巧, 名聲, 諾貝爾獎永續制度等

- 避免把房子蓋在沙子上, 如假神, 壞書籍, 損友, 錯誤的工作技巧, 無益的解決方式等

Characters of Coney

- Little power

- Make home in the crag.

Lessons can be learnt by human being

- Identify all crags in life such as God, bible, friend, exam skills, study skills, work skills, reputation, Nobel prize mechanism and so on.

- Avoid to build the house on the sand such as false God, bad books, bad friends, wrong skills, no good solutions and so on.

蝗蟲的特色

-沒有國王;但群體有次序的往前進

-每隻都是平等的;它們可以進行群體決策卻無領導者

-許多種鳥類依序騰空起飛,不會碰撞(如:紅鶴,白鷺絲)

-許多種魚類依序游開或前進,但不會碰撞(如:沙丁魚)

人們可學習的地方(學習哲學)

-採用新方法經營公司,即無老闆模式;組織單位運作,但卻無領導者

-採用國王制度並不是一個好的模式,因為百姓的兒子或女兒必需為國王服務或爭戰;而且國王會從人民中拿取最好的東西供自己使用

Characters of Locust

- No king. But they advance together in ranks.

- Each one is equal. They make group decision without leader.

- Many kind of birds lift or fly in sequence without collision. Ex: Flamingo or Egret.

- Many kind of fishes swim in sequence without collision. Ex: Sardine.

Lessons can be learnt by human being

- Take a new way to run a business without a boss. A organization works without a leader.

- Having a king system is not good because people's sons or daughters have to serve him and fight for him. King will take the best things from people for his own use.

守宮的特色

-體型小及力量微小

-能被抓在手上

-能夠住皇宮,自由進出

-能在牆上行走及隨時聽到屋內的任何談話

人們可學習的地方(學習哲學)

-製作產品或提供服務,能夠被重要人物或一般人
每天使用到

-成為一個可以被重要人物或一般人信任的人

Characters of Lizard

- Small and little strength.

- It can be caught in hand.

- It can live in king's palace and walk in/out freely.

- It can walk on the wall and hear any word in house all the time.

Lessons can be learnt by human being

- Make a product or service needed by somebody or nobody every day.

- Became a person trusted by somebody or nobody.

螞蟻的特色

- 體型微小暨力氣微小
- 勤奮、勤勞
- 在夏日儲存糧食
- 團隊合作
- 階層式結構
- 使用化學物質攻擊敵人
- 在我們週遭環境無所不在

人們可學習的地方(學習哲學)

- 工作努力 & 不偷懶
- 找出不同事件的冬天並且盡早準備(例:考試日期,專案截止日等)
- 樂於與他人合作進而產生良好團隊
- 在每個工作崗位上善盡職責
- 待人有禮
- 先求無所不在,再求獲利

Characters of Ants

- Small & little strength

- Diligent

- Store up food in the summer

- Teamwork

- Hierarchical structure

- Use chemical compound to attack enemy or leave message

- They are ubiquitous in our environment.

Lessons can be learnt by human being

- Work hard & Not lazy

- Identify what is our winter and prepare it early (Ex: exam date, project
deadline and so on.)

- Cooperate with others to become a good team

- Play the role and do job well in the current position.

- Polite to contact with others

- Ubiquitous firstly, then profit.

沙番(岩蹄兔)的特色

- 軟弱的生物
- 把家蓋在磐石中

人們可學習的地方(學習哲學)

-尋找出人生中的每一項磐石,如真神,聖經,益友,考試技巧,學習技巧,工作技巧,名聲,諾貝爾獎永續制度等
- 避免把房子蓋在沙子上,如假神,壞書籍,損友,錯誤的工作技巧,無益的解決方式等

Characters of Coney

- Little power
- Make home in the crag.

Lessons can be learnt by human being

- Identify all crags in life such as God, bible, friend, exam skills, study skills, work skills, reputation, Nobel prize mechanism and so on.
- Avoid to build the house on the sand such as false God, bad books, bad friends, wrong skills, no good solutions and so on.

螳螂的特色

-沒有國王;但群體有次序的往前進

-每隻都是平等的;它們可以進行群體決策卻無領導者

-許多種鳥類依序騰空起飛,不會碰撞(如:紅鶴,白鷺絲)

-許多種魚類依序游開或前進,但不會碰撞(如:沙丁魚)

人們可學習的地方(學習哲學)

-採用新方法經營公司,即無老闆模式;組織單位運作,但卻無領導者

-採用國王制度並不是一個好的模式,

因為百姓的兒子或女兒必需為國王服務或爭戰;

而且國王會從人民中拿取最好的東西供自已使用

Characters of Locust

- No king. But they advance together in ranks.

- Each one is equal. They make group decision without leader.

- Many kind of birds lift or fly in sequence without collision.
Ex:Flamingo or Egret.

- Mank kind of fishes swim in sequence without collision. Ex: Sardine.

Lessons can be learnt by human being

- Take a new way to run a business without a boss. A organization
works wighout a leader.

- Having a king system is not good because people's sons or
daughters have to serve him and fight for him. King will take the best
things from people for his own use.

守宮的特色

-體型小及力量微小

-能被抓在手上

-能夠住皇宮,自由進出

-能在牆上行走及隨時聽到屋內的任何談話

人們可學習的地方(學習哲學)

-製作產品或提供服務,能夠被重要人物或一般人每天使用到

-成為一個可以被重要人物或一般人信任的人

Characters of Lizard

- Small and little strength
- It can be caught in hand.
- It can live in king's palace and walk in/out freely.
- It can walk on the wall and hear any word in house all the time.

Lessons can be learnt by human being

- Make a product or service needed by somebody or nobody everyday.
- Became a person trusted by somebody or nobody.

CHAPTER V. **Ostrich**

The Lord Answers Job - Ostrich Topic

- Job 38:1-2,39:13-18 (NIV)(New International Version)

1. Then out of the storm the Lord spoke to Job.

2. Who are you to question my wisdom

   with your ignorant, empty words?

3. The wings of the ostrich flap joyfully,

   though they cannot compare with the wings and feathers of
the stork.

4. She lays her eggs on the ground

   and lets them warm in the sand,

5. unmindful that a foot may crush them,

   that some wild animal may trample them.

6. She treats her young harshly, as if they were not hers;

   she cares not that her labor was in vain,

7. for God did not endow her with wisdom

   or give her a share of good sense.

8. Yet when she spreads her feathers to run, she laughs at horse
and rider.

The Lord Answers Job - Ostrich Topic

- Job 38:1-2,39:13-18 (GNT)(Good News Translation)

1. Who is this that obscures my plans

   with words without knowledge?

2. How fast the wings of an ostrich beat!

   But no ostrich can fly like a stork.

3. The ostrich leaves her eggs on the ground

   for the heat in the soil to warm them.

4. She is unaware that a foot may crush them

   or a wild animal break them.

5. She acts as if the eggs were not hers,

   and is unconcerned that her efforts were wasted.

6. It was I who made her foolish

   and did not give her wisdom.

7. But when she begins to run,

   she can laugh at any horse and rider.

耶和華以造物之妙詰約伯-鴕鳥篇

-約伯記 38:1-2,39:13-18（CUVMPT）

Chinese Union Version Modern Punctuation
(Traditional)

1. 那時，耶和華從旋風中回答約伯說：

2. 誰用無知的言語，使我的旨意暗昧不明？

3. 鴕鳥的翅膀歡然搧展，豈是顯慈愛的翎毛和羽毛嗎？

4. 因牠把蛋留在地上，在塵土中使得溫暖，

5. 卻想不到被腳踹碎，或被野獸踐踏。

6. 牠忍心待雛，似乎不是自己的；雖然徒受勞苦，也不為雛懼怕。

7. 因為神使牠沒有智慧，也未將悟性賜給牠。

8. 牠幾時挺身展開翅膀，就嗤笑馬和騎馬的人。

耶和華以造物之妙詰約伯-鴕鳥篇

-约伯记 38:1-2,39:13-18(CCB)

Chinese Contemporary Bible (Simplified)

1. 那时，耶和华从旋风中回答约伯说：

2. 是是谁用无知的话蒙蔽我的旨意？

3. 鸵鸟欢然拍动翅膀，它岂有白鹳的翎羽？

4. 它将蛋产在地上，使蛋得到沙土的温暖，

5. 却不知蛋会被踩碎，或遭野兽践踏。

6. 它苛待雏鸟，好像它们并非己出，就算徒劳一场，它也不怕。

7. 因为上帝未赐它智慧，没有给它悟性。

8. 然而，一旦它展翅奔跑，必嗤笑马儿和骑士。

1. Then out of the storm the Lord spoke to Job.

2. Who are you to question my wisdom with your ignorant, empty words?

1. 那時，耶和華從旋風中回答約伯說：

2. 誰用無知的言語，使我的旨意暗昧不明？

3. The wings of the ostrich flap joyfully, though they cannot
compare with the wings and feathers of the stork.

3. 鴕鳥的翅膀歡然搧展，豈是顯慈愛的翎毛和羽毛嗎？

4. She lays her eggs on the ground and lets them warm in the sand.

4. 因牠把蛋留在地上，在塵土中使得溫暖

5. unmindful that a foot may crush them,

that some wild animal may trample them.

5. 卻想不到被腳踹碎，或被野獸踐踏。

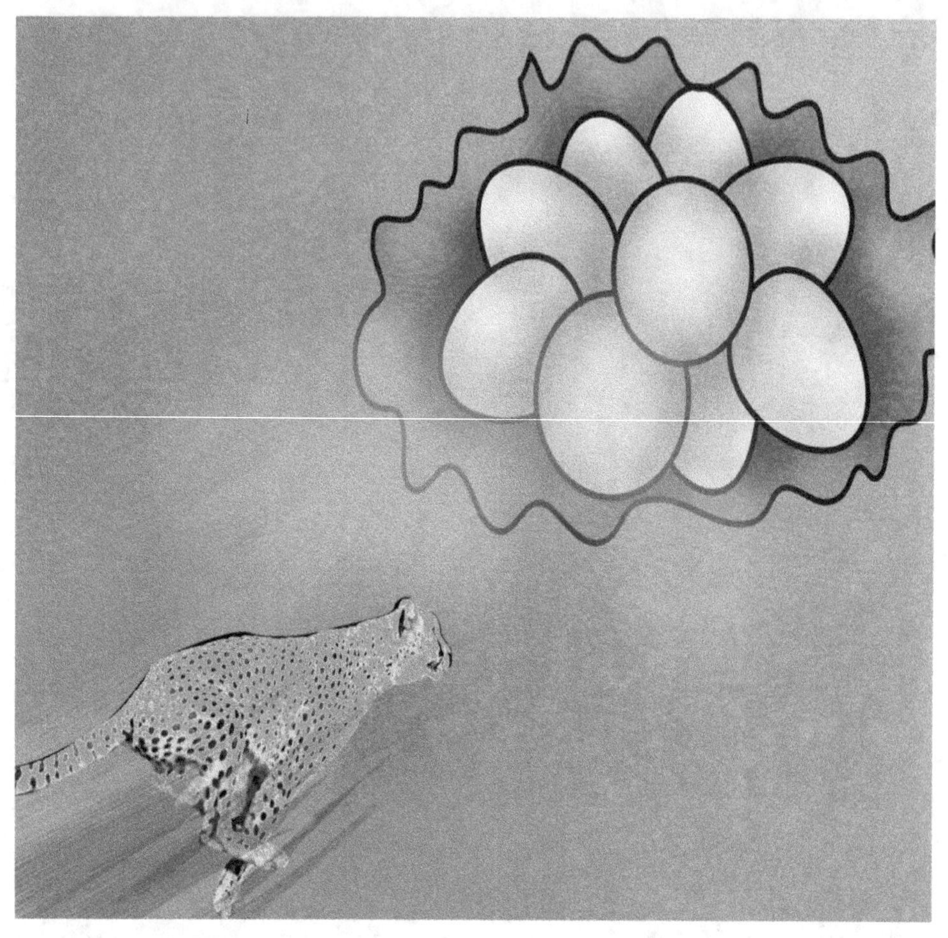

6. She treats her young harshly, as if they were not hers;

she cares not that her labor was in vain

6. 牠忍心待雛，似乎不是自己的；雖然徒受勞苦，也不為雛懼怕。

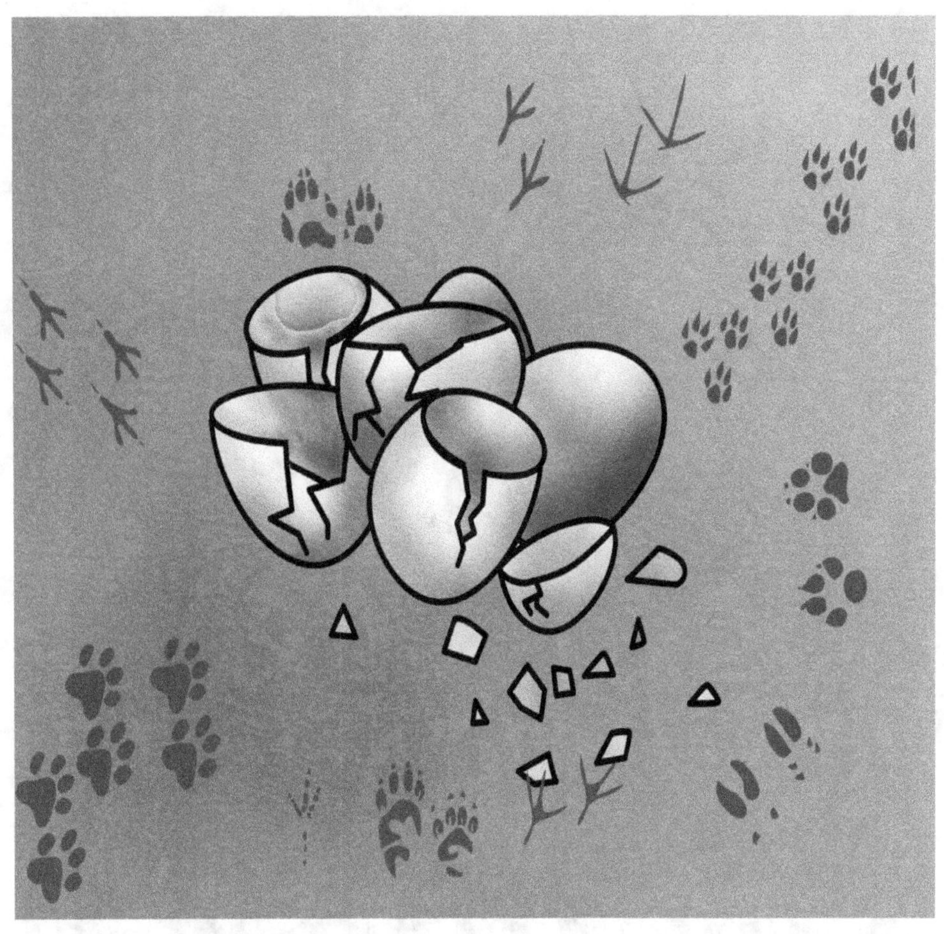

7. for God did not endow her with wisdom or give her a share of good sense.

7. 因為神使牠沒有智慧，也未將悟性賜給牠。

8. Yet when she spreads her feathers to run, she laughs at horse and rider.

8. 牠幾時挺身展開翅膀，就嗤笑馬和騎馬的人。

駝鳥的特色

-把蛋下在土上, 用砂子暖蛋

-漠不關心, 其它動物踩碎蛋

-粗糙或粗暴地地對待自己的孩子

-不在乎自己所作的事變成虛空

-愚笨, 不聰明

-奔跑快過於大多數的馬

人們可學習的地方（學習哲學）

-避免愚昧行為（轉離與改變）

-瞭解與探索個人的天賦

-充份發揮個人的天份

-不要讓個人所作的工變成虛空

-時常跟 神禱告求聰明智慧

Characters of Ostrich

-Lay eggs on the ground and let sand warm them.

-It was so careless that animal may crush eggs.

-Treat her kids harshly.

-Does not care that her labor was in vain.

-Stupid. No smart.

-Faster than most horses.

Lessons can be learnt by human being

-Avoid being a fool. (Turn and Change)

-Explore personal talent.

-Take full advantage of personal talent.

-Don't let our labors be in vain.

-Pray for wisdom from GOD all the time

駝鳥的特色

-把蛋下在土上,用砂子暖蛋
-漠不關心,其它動物踩碎蛋
-粗糙或粗暴地地對待自已的孩子
-不在乎自已所作的事變成虛空
-愚笨,不聰明
-奔跑快過於大多數的馬

人們可學習的地方(學習哲學)

-避免愚昧行為(轉離與改變)
-瞭解與探索個人的天賦
-充份發揮個人的天份
-不要讓個人所作的工變成虛空
-時常跟 神禱告求聰明智慧

Characters of Ostrich

-Lay eggs on the ground and let sand warm them.
-It was so careless that animal may crush eggs.
-Treat her kids harshly.
-Does not care that her labor was in vain.
-Stupid. No smart.
-Faster than most horses.

Lessons can be learnt by human being

-Avoid being a fool. (Turn and Change)
-Explore personal talent.
-Take full advantage of personal talent.
-Don't let our labors be in vain.
-Pray for wisdom from GOD all the time.

CHAPTER VI. **Wild OX**

The Lord Answers Job - Wild Ox Topic

-Job 39:9-12 (NIV) New International Version

1.Will the wild ox consent to serve you?

  Will it stay by your manger at night?

2. Can you hold it to the furrow with a harness?

  Will it till the valleys behind you?

3. Will you rely on it for its great strength?

  Will you leave your heavy work to it?

4. Can you trust it to haul in your grain

  and bring it to your threshing floor?

The Lord Answers Job - Wild Ox Topic

-Job 39:9-12 (GNT) Good News Translation

1. Will a wild ox work for you?

  Is he willing to spend the night in your stable?

2. Can you hold one with a rope and make him plow?

  Or make him pull a harrow in your fields?

3. Can you rely on his great strength

  and expect him to do your heavy work?

4. Do you expect him to bring in your harvest

  and gather the grain from your threshing place?

耶和華以造物之妙詰約伯-野牛篇

約伯記 39:9-12 (CUVMPT)

Chinese Union Version Modern Punctuation
(Traditional)

1.野牛豈肯服侍你？豈肯住在你的槽旁？

2.你豈能用套繩將野牛籠在犁溝之間？牠豈肯隨你耙山谷之地？

3.豈可因牠的力大就倚靠牠？豈可把你的工交給牠做嗎？

4.豈可信靠牠把你的糧食運到家，又收聚你禾場上的穀嗎？

约伯记 39:9-12 (CCB)

Chinese Contemporary Bible (Simplified)

1.野牛岂肯为你效劳，在你的槽旁过夜？

2.你岂能用缰绳把野牛牵到犁沟？它岂肯跟着你在山谷耕地？

3.你岂能倚靠它的大力，把你的重活交给它？

4.岂能靠它运回粮食，替你堆聚到麦场？

1. Will the wild ox consent to serve you? Will it stay by your manger at night?

1. 野牛豈肯服侍你？豈肯住在你的槽旁？

2. Can you hold it to the furrow with a harness?

   Will it till the valleys behind you?

2. 你豈能用套繩將野牛籠在犁溝之間？牠豈肯隨你耙山谷
   之地？

3. Will you rely on it for its great strength?

   Will you leave your heavy work to it?

3. 豈可因牠的力大就倚靠牠？

   豈可把你的工交給牠做嗎？

4. Can you trust it to haul in your grain and bring it to your threshing floor?

4. 豈可信靠牠把你的糧食運到家，又收聚你禾場上的穀嗎？

野牛的特色

– 有蠻力。

– 不能依賴他來服務我們。

– 不可被信賴及不穩靠。

– 不能用套繩將野牛籠在犁溝犁田。

人們可學習的地方（學習哲學）

– 不要雇用不可被信任及不穩靠的人，即使他或她有不錯的專業技能。

例：不要雇用會將程式碼加密的程式設計師，即使他的程式能力非常佳。

– 思考問題 1：在您的周圍附近，誰的個性最像野牛呢？

– 思考問題 2：您有野牛的個性嗎？若有的話，要如何矯正呢？

Characters of Wild Ox

- Great Strength.

- Cannot rely on him to bring gain or serve us.

- Not trustable and not reliable.

- Cannot hold him to the furrow with a harness.

Lessons can be learnt by human being

- Don't hire the persons who are not trustable and reliable, even he or she has good skills.

Ex: Don't hire a programmer with outstanding skills but he would encrypt all his codes. That is because it would be no way or difficult to make codes maintainable in the future.

- Think 1: Who is the wild ox near you?

- Think 2: Do you have the character of wild ox? How can you correct it if you do?

野牛的特色

- 有蠻力。
- 不能依賴他來服務我們。
- 不可被信賴及不穩靠。
- 不能用套繩將野牛籠在犁溝犁田。

人們可學習的地方（學習哲學）

- 不要雇用不可被信任及不穩靠的人，即使他或她有不錯的專業技能。
例：不要雇用會將程式碼加密的程式設計師，即使他的程式能力非常佳。
- 思考問題1：在您的周圍附近，誰的個性最像野牛呢？
- 思考問題2：您有野牛的個性嗎？若有的話，要如何矯正呢？

Characters of Wild Ox

- Great Strength.
- Cannot rely on him to bring gain or serve us.
- Not trustable and not reliable.
- Cannot hold him to the furrow with a harness.

Lessons can be learnt by human being

- Don't hire the persons who are not trustable and reliable, even he or she has good skills.
Ex: Don't hire a programmer with outstanding skills but he would encrypt all his codes. Because it would be no way or difficult to make codes maintainable in the future.
- Think 1: Who is the wild ox near you?
- Think 2: Do you have the character of wild ox? How can you correct it if you do?

CHAPTER VII. **Wild Donkey**

The Lord Answers Job - Wild Donkey Topic

-Job 39:5-8 (NIV) New International Version

1. Who let the wild donkey go free? Who untied its ropes?

2. I gave it the wasteland as its home, the salt flats as its habitat.

3. It laughs at the commotion in the town; it does not hear a driver's shout.

4. It ranges the hills for its pasture and searches for any green thing.

____

The Lord Answers Job - Wild Donkey Topic

-Job 39:5-8 (GNT) Good News Translation

1. Who gave the wild donkeys their freedom?

   Who turned them loose and let them roam?

2. I gave them the desert to be their home,

   and let them live on the salt plains.

3. They keep far away from the noisy cities,

   and no one can tame them and make them work.

4. The mountains are the pastures where they feed,

   where they search for anything green to eat.

耶和華以造物之妙詰約伯-野驢篇

約伯記 39:5-8 (CUVMPT)

Chinese Union Version Modern Punctuation (Traditional)

1. 誰放野驢出去自由？誰解開快驢的繩索？

2. 我使曠野做牠的住處，使鹹地當牠的居所。

3. 牠嗤笑城內的喧嚷，不聽趕牲口的喝聲。

4. 遍山是牠的草場，牠尋找各樣青綠之物。

约伯记 39:5-8 (CCB)

Chinese Contemporary Bible (Simplified)

1. 谁让野驴逍遥自在？谁解开了它的缰绳？

2. 我使它以旷野为家，以盐地作居所。

3. 它嗤笑城邑的喧闹，不听赶牲口的吆喝。

4. 它以群山作草场，寻找青翠之物。

1. Who let the wild donkey go free? Who untied its ropes?

1. 誰放野驢出去自由？誰解開快驢的繩索？

2. I gave it the wasteland as its home, the salt flats as its habitat.

2. 我使曠野做牠的住處，使鹹地當牠的居所。

3. It laughs at the commotion in the town; it does not hear a driver's shout.

3. 牠嗤笑城內的喧嚷，不聽趕牲口的喝聲。

4. It ranges the hills for its pasture and searches for any green thing.

4. 遍山是牠的草場，牠尋找各樣青綠之物。

野驢的特色

- 視荒地為家, 隨遇而安。

- 不斷尋找青綠色的東西。

- 聽不見趕牲口的喝聲。

- 喜歡自由, 牧場地與青綠事物。

- 遍山是牠的草場。

人們可學習的地方（學習哲學）

- 享受自由的馳聘心靈與身軀。

- 享受鄉間生活, 超過城市。

- 享受自由的研究生活。

- 嘗試自我雇用生活方式。

- 經常遠望青綠事物, 以保護眼睛。

- 設定心智經常尋找智慧與 神。

Characters of wild donkey

- See wasteland as its home.

- Search for the green thing.

- Don't hear a driver's shout.

- Love freedom, pasture and green things.

- Range the hills for the pasture.

Lessons can be learnt by human being

- Enjoy the freedom of mind and body.

- Enjoy the life in country more than city.

- Enjoy the research and development life.

- Try the self-employment life style.

- See more green things to protect eyes every day.

- Search for wisdom and GOD all the time.

野驢的特色

- 視荒地為家, 隨遇而安。
- 不斷尋找青綠色的東西。
- 聽不見趕牲口的喝聲。
- 喜歡自由, 牧場地與青綠事物。
- 遍山是牠的草場。

人們可學習的地方(學習哲學)

- 享受自由的馳騁心靈與身軀。
- 享受鄉間生活, 超過城市。
- 享受自由的研究生活。
- 嘗試自我雇用生活方式。
- 經常遠望青綠事物, 以保護眼睛。
- 設定心智經常尋找智慧與 神。

Characters of wild donkey

- See wasteland as its home.
- Search for the green thing.
- Don't hear a driver's shout.
- Love freedom, pasture and green things.
- Range the hills for the pasture.

Lessons can be learnt by human being

- Enjoy the freedom of mind and body.
- Enjoy the life in country more than city.
- Enjoy the research and development life.
- Try the self-employment life style.
- See more green things to protect eyes every day.
- Search for wisdom and GOD all the time.

CHAPTER VIII. Weeds Parable

The Parable of the Weeds

Matthew 13:24-30 (NIV) New International Version

1. Jesus told them another parable: The kingdom of heaven is like a man who sowed good seed in his field.

2. But while everyone was sleeping, his enemy came and sowed weeds among the wheat, and went away.

3. When the wheat sprouted and formed heads, then the weeds also appeared.

4. The owner's servants came to him and said, Sir, didn't you sow good seed in your field? Where then did the weeds come from?

5. An enemy did this, he replied.

The servants asked him, Do you want us to go and pull them up?

6. No, he answered, because while you are pulling the weeds, you may uproot the wheat with them.

7. Let both grow together until the harvest. At that time I will tell the harvesters: First collect the weeds and tie them in bundles to be burned; then gather the wheat and bring it into my barn.

The Parable of the Weeds

Matthew 13:24-30 (GNT) Good News Translation

1. Jesus told them another parable: The Kingdom of heaven is like this. A man sowed good seed in his field.

2. One night, when everyone was asleep, an enemy came and sowed weeds among the wheat and went away.

3. When the plants grew and the heads of grain began to form, then the weeds showed up.

4. The man's servants came to him and said, Sir, it was good seed you sowed in your field; where did the weeds come from?

5. It was some enemy who did this, he answered. Do you want us to go and pull up the weeds? they asked him.

6. No, he answered, because as you gather the weeds you might pull up some of the wheat along with them.

7. Let the wheat and the weeds both grow together until harvest. Then I will tell the harvest workers to pull up the weeds first, tie them in bundles and burn them, and then to gather in the wheat and put it in my barn.

稗子的比喻

馬太福音 13:24-30（CUVMPT）

Chinese Union Version Modern Punctuation
(Traditional)

1. 耶穌又設個比喻對他們說：天國好像人撒好種在田裡，

2. 及至人睡覺的時候，有仇敵來，將稗子撒在麥裡就走了。

3. 到長苗吐穗的時候，稗子也顯出來。

4. 田主的僕人來告訴他說：『主啊，你不是撒好種在田裡嗎？從哪裡來的稗子呢？』

5. 主人說：『這是仇敵做的。』僕人說：『你要我們薅出來嗎？』

6. 主人說：不必，恐怕薅稗子，連麥子也拔出來。

7. 容這兩樣一齊長，等著收割。當收割的時候，我要對收割的人說：先將稗子薅出來，捆成捆，留著燒，唯有麥子要收在倉裡。

毒麦的比喻

马太福音 13:24-30（CCB）

Chinese Contemporary Bible（Simplified）

1. 耶稣又给他们讲了一个比喻，说：天国就像一个人，将好种子撒在田里。

2. 人们睡觉的时候，仇敌过来把毒麦撒在他的麦田里，就走了。

3. 当麦子长苗吐穗时，毒麦也长起来了。

4. 奴仆看见了就来问主人，主人啊！你不是把好种子撒在田里了吗？从哪里来的毒麦呢？

5. 主人回答说，这是仇敌做的。奴仆问道，要我们去拔掉它们吗？

6. 主人说，不用了，因为拔毒麦会连麦子一起拔掉。

7. 让它们跟麦子一起生长吧，到收割的时候，我会吩咐收割的工人先把毒麦收集起来，扎成捆，留着烧，然后将麦子存入谷仓。

1. Jesus told them another parable: The kingdom of heaven is like a man who sowed good seed in his field.

1. 耶穌又設個比喻對他們說：天國好像人撒好種在田裡

2. But while everyone was sleeping, his enemy came and sowed weeds among the wheat, and went away.

2. 及至人睡覺的時候，有仇敵來，將稗子撒在麥裡就走了。

3. When the wheat sprouted and formed heads, then the weeds also appeared.

3. 到長苗吐穗的時候，稗子也顯出來。

4. The owner's servants came to him and said, Sir, didn't you sow good seed in your field? Where then did the weeds come from?

4. 田主的僕人來告訴他說：『主啊，你不是撒好種在田裡嗎？從哪裡來的稗子呢？』

5. An enemy did this, he replied. The servants asked him,

Do you want us to go and pull them up?

5. 主人說：『這是仇敵做的。』僕人說：『你要我們薅出來嗎？』

6. No, he answered, because while you are pulling the weeds, you may uproot the wheat with them.

6. 主人說：不必，恐怕薅稗子，連麥子也拔出來。

7. Let both grow together until the harvest. At that time I will tell the harvesters: First collect the weeds and tie them in bundles to be burned; then gather the wheat and bring it into my barn.

7. 容這兩樣一齊長，等著收割。當收割的時候，我要對收割的人說：先將稗子薅出來，捆成捆，留著燒，唯有麥子要收在倉裡。

稗子的特色

-稗子是惡者的後裔

-稗子在**收割時**將被會被拔起與燒毀

-稗子會被**收割者**拔起與燒毀

-播種稗子的敵人是惡者

人們可學習的地方(學習哲學)

-在我們身心靈裡要成長麥子(好事)及停止成長稗子(壞事)

-學習麥子使世界獲益,拒學稗子讓世界腐敗

-嘗試當一個好麥子,而非壞稗子

-避免讓原本好的事物變成壞事物(如:福斯汽車員工利用電腦欺騙排放測試)

-嘗試將原本壞的事物變成好事物(如:垃圾變黃金,苦煉樹籽提煉油後的殘渣可處理成有機肥料)

-在每個人的幼童時期都有純潔的心靈,但部份人在成長過程中逐漸腐壞它

Characters of Weeds

-The weeds are the sons of the evil one.

-Weeds will be pulled up and burned in the fire at the harvest time.

-Weeds will be pulled up and burned in the fire by harvesters.

-The enemy who sows weeds is the devil.

Lesson can be learnt by human being

-Grow wheat (good things) and stop weed(bad things) in our mind and heart.

-Learn wheat to benefit the world but not learn weed to corrupt the world.

-To be like a good wheat instead of a bad weed.

-Prevent turning good things into bad things. (Ex: Volkswagen employee use computer to cheat emissions tests)

-Try to turn something bad into something good. (Ex: Turn garbage into gold. Residue of neem seeds after oil extraction can be processed into a natural fertilizer.)

-Good minds begin in the period of infancy for everyone, but some corrupt them when they grow up.

稗子的特色

-稗子是惡者的後裔
-稗子在收割時將被會被拔起與燒毀
-稗子會被收割者拔起與燒毀
-播種稗子的敵人是惡者

人們可學習的地方(學習哲學)

-在我們身心靈裡要成長麥子(好事)及停止成長稗子(壞事)
-學習麥子使世界獲益,拒學稗子讓世界腐敗
-嘗試當一個好麥子,而非壞稗子
-避免讓原本好的事物變成壞事物(如:福斯汽車員工利用電腦欺騙排放測試)
-嘗試將原本壞的事物變成好事物(如:垃圾變黃金,苦煉樹籽提煉油後的殘渣可處理成有機肥料)
-在每個人的幼童時期都有純潔的心靈,但部份人在成長過程中逐漸腐壞它

Characters of Weeds

-The weeds are the sons of the evil one.
-Weeds will be pulled up and burned in the fire at the harvest time.
-Weeds will be pulled up and burned in the fire by harvesters.
-The enemy who sows weeds is the devil.

Lesson can be learnt by human being

-Grow wheat(good things) and stop weed(bad things) in our mind and heart.
-Learn wheat to benefit the world but not learn weed to corrupt the world.
-To be like a good wheat instead of a bad weed.
-Prevent turning good things into bad things. (Ex: Volkswagen employee use computer to cheat emissions tests)
-Try to turn something bad into something good. (Ex: Turn garbage into gold. Residue of neem seeds after oil extraction can be processed into a natural fertilizer.)
-Good minds begin in the period of infancy for everyone, but some corrupt them when they grow up.

CHAPTER IX. **Sower Parable**

The Parable of the Sower
Mark 4:3-8 (NIV) New International Version

1. Listen! Once there was a man who went out to sow grain.
2. As he scattered the seed in the field, some of it fell along the path, and the birds came and ate it up.
3. Some of it fell on rocky ground, where there was little soil. The seeds soon sprouted, because the soil wasn't deep.
4. Then, when the sun came up, it burned the young plants; and because the roots had not grown deep enough, the plants soon dried up.
5. Some of the seed fell among thorn bushes, which grew up and choked the plants, and they didn't bear grain.
6. But some seeds fell in good soil, and the plants sprouted, grew, and bore grain: some had thirty grains, others sixty, and others one hundred.

The Parable of the Sower
Mark 4:3-8 (GNT) Good News Translation

1. Listen! Once there was a man who went out to sow grain.
2. As he scattered the seed in the field, some of it fell along the path, and the birds came and ate it up.
3. Some of it fell on rocky ground, where there was little soil. The seeds soon sprouted, because the soil wasn't deep.
4. Then, when the sun came up, it burned the young plants; and because the roots had not grown deep enough, the plants soon dried up.
5. Some of the seed fell among thorn bushes, which grew up and choked the plants, and they didn't bear grain.
6. But some seeds fell in good soil, and the plants sprouted, grew, and bore grain: some had thirty grains, others sixty, and others one hundred.

撒種的比喻
馬可福音 4:3-8 (CUVMPT)

Chinese Union Version Modern Punctuation (Traditional)
1.你們聽啊！有一個撒種的出去撒種。
2.撒的時候，有落在路旁的，飛鳥來吃盡了。
3.有落在土淺石頭地上的，土既不深，發苗最快，
4.日頭出來一曬，因為沒有根，就枯乾了。
5.有落在荊棘裡的，荊棘長起來，把它擠住了，就不結實。

6.又有落在好土裡的，就發生長大，結實有三十倍的，
有六十倍的，有一百倍的。

撒种的比喻
马可福音 4:3-8 (CCB)

Chinese Contemporary Bible (Simplified)
1.听着！有一个农夫出去撒种。
2.撒种的时候，有些种子落在路旁，被飞鸟吃掉了；
3.有些落在石头地上，因为泥土不深，种子很快就发芽了，

4.然而因为没有根，被太阳一晒就枯萎了；
5.有些落在荆棘丛中，荆棘长起来便把嫩苗挤住了，以致
不能结实；
6.有些落在沃土里，就发芽生长，结出果实，
收成多达三十倍、六十倍、一百倍！

1. Listen! Once there was a man who went out to sow grain.

1. 你們聽啊！有一個撒種的出去撒種。

2. As he scattered the seed in the field, some of it fell along the path, and the birds came and ate it up.

2. 撒的時候，有落在路旁的，飛鳥來吃盡了。

3. Some of it fell on rocky ground, where there was little soil.
The seeds soon sprouted, because the soil wasn't deep.

3. 有落在土淺石頭地上的，土既不深，發苗最快，

4. Then, when the sun came up, it burned the young plants; and because the roots had not grown deep enough, the plants soon dried up.

4. 日頭出來一曬，因為沒有根，就枯乾了。

5. Some of the seed fell among thorn bushes, which grew up and choked the plants, and they didn't bear grain.

5.有落在荊棘裡的，荊棘長起來，把它擠住了，就不結實。

6. But some seeds fell in good soil, and the plants sprouted, grew, and bore grain: some had thirty grains, others sixty, and others one hundred.

6. 又有落在好土裡的，就發生長大，結實有三十倍的，有六十倍的，有一百倍的。

撒種者及種子的特色

-撒種者:農夫, 每人, 教師, 媒體, 政治家

-種子:植物, 知識, 行為, 技能

-種子會偵測環境, 並決定發芽時間點(門檻值達到時)

-所有成長所需軟硬體都被封裝在一顆顆的小種子空間裡面

人們可學習的地方(學習哲學)

-學生在教室聽及學知識

-我們在各領域常需扮演學生的角色與心態

-讓我們自己本身成為好的土壤, 以利隨時接受新知識

-把種子播到好土壤(好學生)

-努力工作使收成從 30 倍增加到 60 倍或更多

-不要等到最佳天氣及風再撒種, 因將無法播出種子

Characters of Sower and Seed

-Sower: Farmer, everyone, teacher, media, politican.

-Seed: Plant, knowledge, behavior, skill.

-Seeds detect environment and decide to sprout if
the threshold is exceeded.

-All software and hardware for growing are packaged
into a small seed.

Lesson can be learnt by human being

-Students listen and learn knowledge in the
classroom.

-We often play the role of student in every field.

-Let myself to be a good soil to learn knowledge
all the time.

-Sow my seed to a good soil (good student).

-Work hard to let harvest jump from 30 to 60 or
more times.

-Do not wait until the perfect wind and weather,
you will never plant.

撒種者及種子的特色

-撒種者:農夫,每人,教師,媒體,政治家
-種子:植物,知識,行為,技能
-種子會偵測環境,並決定發芽時間點(門檻值達到時)
-所有成長所需軟硬體都被封裝在一顆顆的小種子空間裡面

人們可學習的地方(學習哲學)

-學生在教室聽及學知識
-我們在各領域常需扮演學生的角色與心態
-讓我們自己本身成為好的土壤,以利隨時接受新知識
-把種子播到好土壤(好學生)
-努力工作使收成從30倍增加到60倍或更多
-不要等到最佳天氣及風再撒種,因將無法播出種子

Characters of Sower and Seed

-Sower: Farmer, everyone, teacher, media, politican
-Seed: Plant, knowledge, behavior, skill
-Seeds detect environment and decide to sprout if the threshold is exceeded.
-All software and hardware for growing are packaged into a small seed.

Lesson can be learnt by human being

-Student listen and learn knowledge in the classroom.
-We often play the role of student in every field.
-Let myself to be a good soil to learn knowledge all the time.
-Sow my seed to a good soil (good student).
-Work hard to let harvest jump from 30 to 60 or more times.
-Do not wait until the perfect wind and weather, you will never plant.

Appendix A. Related Android App

The related app for some contents of this book in
the Google Play store can be freely downloaded.

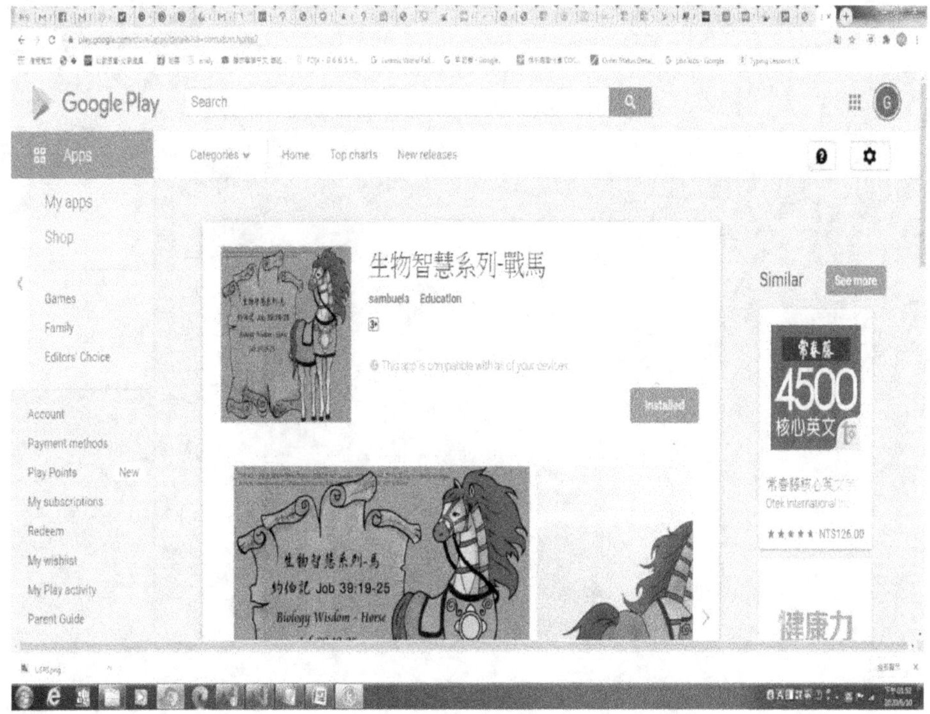